Indie Excellence
FINALIST
Book Awards

An Agreement
with Love

Enjoy,
Kristina Mercier
Jul 2011

An Agreement with Love

Opening to the Flow of Life

KRISTINA RENEE MERCIER

Stella Loretta
PUBLISHING
Baltimore, MD

An Agreement with Love
Opening to the Flow of Life

Published by

Stella Loretta
PUBLISHING

To order additional copies go to:
www.kristinamercier.com or
www.anagreementwithlove.com

Cover design by Peri Poloni-Gabriel, Knockout Design, www.knockoutbooks.com

Interior design and layout by Peri Poloni-Gabriel, Knockout Design, www.knockoutbooks.com and Dorie McClelland, Spring Book Design

Author Photo by Bonnie Johnson Photography

ISBN: 978-0-6153553-7-5
LCCN: 2010908756

Publisher's Cataloging-In-Publication Data
(Prepared by The Donohue Group, Inc.)

Mercier, Kristina Renee.
  An agreement with love : opening to the flow of life / Kristina Renee Mercier.
-- 1st ed.

  p. : ill. ; cm.

  ISBN: 978-0-615-35537-5

  1. Conduct of life. 2. Self-realization. 3. Love. 4. American literature-- Women authors. I. Title.

PS3613.E735 A47 2010
818.6/08
2010908756

First Edition

Printed in the United States of America

Dedicated to

Charles and Barbara Mercier

*Thank you
for raising me in love.*

Dear Red,

That book of love, the one you are having the courage to write. You've been writing so long. Know it's about all of us. Write on.

Keep your head down, your heart open, and write on. It will finish.

Blue Morpho

An Agreement with Love

In the beginning,
Love offered a choice.

It said, "Let me swim in you.
Let me dive from a high cliff

into the deep blue of your soul.
Let me merge easily

with the wellspring of your life,
taking full possession of you.

For this, I will fill
your days and nights with Love

and if you let me
flow through you now,

I will never leave you.
I will always be with you,

though this life
will surely take its toll."

So I opened up,
and I let love in.

Chapter One

On This Day

I remember the day.
It was the one
that could last forever.

Like one lover curled
around another,
sated.

It was the day
I prayed for,
to kneel

side by side with him
and make our vows
to believe

that on this day,
we can last
forever.

My Vows

I will be the wood,
if you will be the nail.
Skimming waves I'll be the hull,
if you will be the sail.

If you will be the shoe,
I will be the lace.
An opaque shade to dim the light
I'll be, if you will be the base.

I will be the band,
and you can shine up on the mount.
A broken gate out in a field I'll be,
if you're an ivy wound around.

To all these things, I'll give my life
as long you're a part combined.
I am the woman, you are the man
to have, and to hold, this one time.

The Picture He Took

I love the picture he took of me
during our trip to the Sleeping Bear
Dunes. It was the day we explored

favorite places. The two-track going nowhere
into the woods. The grimy pub to share
a beer with the locals. The living room floor

where we made love. The beach.
I walked on the dunes while he perfected
a shot of me against the landscape

of sand falling away
into Lake Michigan's shore
far below. Out on the horizon the waves

rolled peacefully and the sun set
into a pastel sky. But all I saw was him.
He was framing the shot, changing the angle,

turning, bending, lying on his back
to get it right. His concentration was beautiful
to me. The way he attended to the details of life

filled me, swelling my heart tight
against my chest, until I struggled
for breath. I was terrified to love

him so deep. It sprung up from a place
where he could never be. "Stop there," he said,
"and look out to the lake." I turned

as the wind blew my hair, veiling my face
that was struggling between unrestrained
love and the fear of being left alone in it.

Click! He smiled, capturing me perfectly.

Waking Next to You

I watch you.
Sleeping like a small boy,
lashes, a thick brush of dark

velvet against your cheek.
I've come to know your temper well,
it drives a veil of silence

over our home.
How I have learned
to soothe your quiet anger

by suppressing myself.
It is the only way to survive
between loving the likeness

of a sweet boy
who breathes so deep
and the caged tiger that wakes,

prowling through a day.
Somewhere in the middle
is the man who loves me.

Casting Off in Crescent City

I watched you cast off
from the docks in Crescent
City. You stood among
the others, lined up against
the rail, the old ones

who'd been casting
off this dock forever.
I was in the distance
because from faraway
I can fall in love

all over again
with your intensity
to know the world.
You were alive
among the old,

wise fisherman
and they beamed
with pride at your attention
to their teachings.
They showed you how

to tie the knots and hook
the bait just right,
so it hung lifelike. They showed
you how to pick your mark
out on the water and find

your perfect release
when casting the pole.
You cast, and cast again,
focusing on the release
and hitting the target,

indifferent to the bait
needing to sink into the sea
to catch your prize.
Suddenly I felt like a fish
in the deep, waiting.

Prayer for a Child

Look at me, your wife,
and give me your promise
that our love will
have a chance to live.

A chance to be a seed
of new life with an innocence
to bend the steel
that has not yet given in you.

I will bear
the consequence
of whatever may come to pass
if this appeal fails.

This is my last prayer.

*People carry their inner torments with them — to work,
to drop off their kids, to meetings, to coffee shops
and street corners.*

I can pick up the scent of sadness everywhere.

*Sometimes, alone with my own pain, wisdom rises
in me. I know the only way to free myself from this
encroaching ache is a complete bursting of the seams
that keeps me hemmed in so tight, I can't breathe.*

*To release this torrent of emotion in me
will change everything I know. It is terrifying,*

but I feel it coming.

The Fall of Love

Lying still and quiet, I feel
you slip between the covers and rest
your head on the pillow, inches from mine.

Even now, I long for your arms
to fold around me. But soon I feel heat
radiate from your back

like the Winter's sun
felt on my face
through the kitchen window

this afternoon. Night time,
when truth is traded for dreams
I can forget I am changing,

I am changed.
I loathe the morning light now
waking me back into the world

where I am the one
who is going to leave you.
During these last days

I've become like the awful,
willful leaf that still clings
to the high branch of our old Oak,

long after the Fall winds
have come and gone. Taunting me
with its own demise.

I wonder if it will come down tomorrow.

There is a tightening in me. Like a vice handle turning by the smallest increments, steadily squeezing out every drop of love left in my heart, preparing me for what is to come.

It is a tiny gesture of compassion that I can't feel love or pain anymore, only constriction; slowly suffocating while overseeing the disintegration of my vows. It is finished.

From the Letter He Wrote

The letter he wrote is kept in
the middle of *The Agony and the Ecstasy*,
his favorite book about Michelangelo.

"I wish
this could be a letter
about love
instead of about good-bye.
But with proceedings underway
I wanted you to know

I've never lost
anyone close to me.
The pain of you leaving
is overwhelming,
especially when I realize
the chance we had to heal.

I am sorry
I didn't give you
what you needed.
You gave me
the first love I ever felt
and now, I am without.

Knowing how I felt
was all you wanted
and I kept it from you,
out of a fear you would know
I'd be lost without you.
Look at me now.

I am mostly sorry
we have no children.
How could I have denied
you, us, that bond?
I will miss your smile,
which is genuine

and your laugh
which is hearty,
and made me whole.
I hope the man
you choose to give them to,
is ready for such a gift.

I love you."

Aftermath

Over a year has passed
and I'm still vacant.

Memories, of me and you,
are kept dormant

because of the fragility
that shakes my skin

if I let one out
and into my mind.

These days I step lightly,
careful to only walk

where we've never been.
Where I am in shadows,

known to no one. Letting go
of life with you

was like my own solitary death,
a choice to crush my chest.

You were all I knew,
and why I thought I lived.

To be born and to die is effortless compared to what we are called to be in between.

Self-Portrait

If I make the lashes
darker and cheeks
more bright, or touch
the lips with hints
of red, would this make up
for my offense?

Or, cast a spell
for mirror to mirror
to reflect a flawless
apparition? Could it sink
into my skin, heal me,
make me new?

What if I rendered myself
from the outside in?
Could I find a path
back to my original place?
Or ever find the face
I had before the choice

to love was made?
No. This transgression
seeps beyond skin
settling inside,
becoming mine. A new
face to know.

Babe and a Bitch

To all eyes she lay peacefully, body
reclined on a striped blanket,
dark glasses hiding scared eyes,
head resting on bunched
up towels, golden curls
falling about, framing lips
longing to speak, to tell her story.

The heat of the sun beat
down on her pale skin, baking
into her, hardening
her heart into a shield.
To move terrified her.
She wanted to rest,
forget that she'd ever loved.

She lay cloaked
in her own darkness.
A man passed.
He said, "Hey Babe."
She remained still, silent,
to which he responded,
"You bitch."

Psalm at the Sea

I tried to remember
when it was I let you go,
but this morning I was filled
only with the darkness
of my turning away.

In the past, a return
to the sea would be enough
for me to find you in powerful
crashing waves, or in trying
to grasp the infinity of sand.

But I am broken, this time,
by the wicked weight I bear
from leaving love
behind. It is so silent,
like the world is drained.

Revival at the Seaside

Open child,
open more
than ever before.

Split open wide
to hear my voice.
I am

in the echo
and the wave.
I am

in each grain
of sand.
I am

in the rustle
of the sea grass,
I am

the sun's heat
on your cheek.
I am

in the call
of the gull.
I am

the delicate
twist
of a seashell.

If you open wide,
you will know,
I am

in you
and you have never
let me go.

The Unraveling

After leaving him
I began the penance
of seaming endless threads

into the surface
of my heart.
With gentle curves,

like small kisses,
I worked to disguise
the damage.

With broad sweeps
of imposing arcs,
I wove flowing hues

of cascading indigo
and ocher across the wounds.
Wrapping my heart

with an exquisite design
so pure looking, and perfect
no one would see

the pain of letting love go.
Now, long after,
I kneel once again,

but this time beside
other saints and sinners,
and pray for the courage

to loosen a thread,
rip the perfect rag,
start a complete

and utter unraveling.
So the world knows
my heart still beats.

Reconciling with Love

Seeing him for the first time advancing
across an empty parking lot, felt
like encountering a lion stalking
the Sahara, lone and fearless.

Thick brown curls, cut tight, shimmered
with touches of red in the sunlight. He moved
in graceful, calculated steps, while mine
were stopped dead in their tracks.

The onslaught of first love grabs
hold tight, and feels so wonderful
and right, you are left only with hope
it can withstand time.

Regret is a state that I can't bear to hold.
It devours me from the inside out if I let
it take over. It is best to suffer the pain
until it is ready to let go.

The gift of our love was the happenstance
of seeing him as he was meant to be seen
in this world, a solitary, beautiful man left wild
in a time with too many rules.

The way it felt to love him is seared into me,
along with our falling apart. Loving him
was my only way to know him. And leaving him
was the only way to know myself.

Weeds

Lying here in the weeds
beneath this tree,
I feel damn good.

The branches are like
a thousand silver swords
against the night sky.

Bending and waving
all at once in the wind,
churning up the heavens,

delighting my mind.
How can I want
anything more than a life

full of imaginings like this,
lying in weeds under a big
moon sky, alone, but so alive.

The Blue Morpho Butterfly Farm

At the butterfly farm I learned
that once a butterfly emerges
from the chrysalis,
it has less than a month to live.
During that time
it is driven to mate as many times
as possible before it dies.
     On reflection,
as I sat in the netted enclosure
filled with floating butterflies
fluttering, living out their three
or so weeks in a cage,
a silver-haired gentlemen
in the group concluded
this fleeting, passion-filled
butterfly life
was very much like our own.
          I agreed.

But I asked him,
my arms outstretched
letting butterflies crawl
all over me, lighting off my fingers,
perching on my palm, watching
as they opened and closed
their blue, delicate wings,
"Do you think there is such a thing
                as a butterfly in love?"

The man, a kindred spirit
I would come to call Blue Morpho,
smiled at me with sage-like
certainty, hands folded
in his lap, a butterfly
on his head, and said,
"I believe I'm looking at one,
                right now."

Dear Blue Morpho,

It was good to hear from you. I've come a long way since the butterfly farm. Thank you for your wise words. I think knowing you may be a gift from the gods.

I'm going to be OK, despite the fact that I have no idea what will become of me on my own. I have a strange feeling I've started myself on some path of destiny. As if something larger may be at work. I am filling with hope, but cautious at the same time. I suppose this is better than being empty.

I've started to write again which is a good sign that I'm coming out of hiding.

Any new travel plans?

Be Well,
Red

Dear Red,

It is good to hear you are feeling hope. Hope is a great place to start. Life has a funny way of leading us around all kinds of experiences and events. Most times we don't understand the point of it all until well afterwards. In my mind, we're not meant to.

In time you'll learn that some of life's greatest experiences begin after everything we thought was good ends. Try trusting yourself, trust in love, again. See where that gets you.

I am off to kayak in the land of a thousand lakes. If I don't capsize and drown, I will write again soon. Smiling?

Your Friend,

Blue Morpho

P.S. Glad to hear you are writing again. The pen saves many souls, including my own. Write on.

A Way to Live

Like this rose
I will live, intimate and deep.
Like the spin and groove
of her slender petals
bound in this bud,
I will interlace passion,
and wonderment,
pressing each moment
of life into my heart.

Just like her coming bloom,
though no eye will see
her bursting forth,
I, too, will explode into the world
and shimmer from the inside
out and to the very edge
of my being, giving
everything I am
to everyone I meet.

As for her withering,
when her full petals fade
and drop away,
even then, like the rose,
I will embrace my sweet fall
from beauty's grace.
And as my end draws near
I will smile in my final days,
having lived just like this rose.

What I Love

Words,
water,
innocence,
wisdom,
a man's hands,
and the scent
of frankincense.

Sailing on
an open sea.
Expression,
compassion,
the sound
of the wind
blowing leaves.

Lips,
eyes,
a big full moon.
Beauty,
adventure,
climbing
sand dunes.

Dance,
trust,
something new.
Disappearing.
Fresh, warm peaches,
toasted bread and
apricot jelly.

Making time.
Brushing off sand.
My arching back.
Holding hands.
Breaking out.
Breaking in.

The aching sound
of violins.
Quiet strength,
sleeping cats,
freedom,
The Great Lakes,
another chance.

Chapter Two

At Sea

It was new love,
after lost love.

It was overwhelming,
unprepared for,

a breath-taking
first glance,

falling down,
heart-wrenching,

utterly impossible,
deeply passionate,

forever to be damned,
never to be resolved, Love.

But I could feel
again.

Dear Blue Morpho,

*Back in the office again, working through exhaustion
and wishing for darkness to curl me up and set me adrift.*

*I'm still drunk from last night and so in love from last week.
I met a man. It happened in an instant. I fell in love with
him as if I'd fallen for him 1000 times before. Can you
imagine that?*

*It was unintended, he isn't mine. But now, this misplaced
love is like a new life let loose in the world, disruptive
and powerful.*

*I saw him again last night. We struggled with desire for
each other, it is so reckless. His russet eyes melted into a
soulful glance that makes me feel like we've known each
other forever. I know what he's thinking. He wishes he never
saw me that day, but he can't look away.*

*My mind wanders over the fantasy that he would come
get me and we'd run away. I remind myself, he never will.
Nor would I go. But I'm sliding farther with his every glance.*

*You're off to Italy tomorrow? Sounds good. Wish I could
join you and save myself, and him, from falling down this
slippery slope.*

Please write to me soon,

Red

Dear Red,

Ahhh, I'm the last one to make pronouncements about love, right or wrong. I've been around for centuries, it seems, and I still don't understand love, except we all want it, need it, and hunger for all the ways it shows up in our lives.

I do believe we all look for the one person we can say, "Yes" to with a relaxed finality that this is the trusted relationship we want as the home base of our lives. Some people find out it is not with the one they are with, and this realization is difficult.

You have a gentle way of bringing yourself into the world with such honesty, without saying a word. It is a burden to bear. Be kind to yourself. You both responded to love. And that is what we are here to do. Love does not have rules or laws. Love just is, and it is always beautiful.

Feeling it is human. Acting on it is a choice, but either way, fighting it will only make it stronger.

From Italy,

Blue Morpho

The Wave

Never,
had I felt the wave of desire
crash down on me
until the day
I saw his face.
Like a new bird
wounded in first flight,
I am left adrift
from a first kiss.
Dragged back
into his arms
then, thrashed
out of his sight.

How Would You Love Me?

Tell me, how would you love me,
if you could love me?

Like a wind washes over a calm sea?
Or a fire enflames a tangle of brush?

Might I be able to charge the gates of life?
Then, crawl into your open arms at night?

What if the world twirled on the edge
of destruction? Would you leave to love me then?

With that one moment back, I'd risk
the consequences from the chance

that just once, you held me like the sun
wraps round a blade of grass.

At the Bookstore Reading about Quarks

Watching the parking lot from way up here, with its cars coming and going, parking, coming and going, makes me think about quantum physics. They say everything is made up of tiny miniscule bits of subatomic energy popping in and out, within some vast sea of chaotic perfection, even me.

It's funny, in a disturbing way, to think we're all just specks of dust blowing around. But where are we? What are we within? What are we without? Where is the end? There can be no end, or beginning, as time stretches across vast space in some grand arc folding over itself.

But, thinking about all this makes me smile, because imagine, here I am a speck of dust in this tremendous, seemingly endless conglomeration of space and time. Just a fleck of color with no intelligence to grasp the infinitude of what this universe is, or isn't, or never was. And just last night, under a big moon sky, another speck looked at me and said, "I love you."

Isn't that amazing? Two specks hurtling through the universe, one choosing a left, one right, one up, one down, then by chance or a perfect positive attraction, cross paths and are brought to a shuddering halt, compelled to settle in space, to dwell in time, just to discover each other.

Sitting up here, looking down at all the cars, coming and going, makes me feel full and fortunate for each speck of dust choosing its path, forging a trail, making perfect chaotic sense of why we are here, of the only thing we are truly meant to find along our way, Love.

Willing Prey

Pull it across my eyes again lover,
our web of loving lies.

Pull it round me quick!
So truth is blinded

and we can have
one reckless hour

to release our primal bodies
into the light.

When You Come By

When you come by
it feels like a fresh breeze
washing across a quiet sea
rippling up waves of feelings
I've never felt before.

My heart skips a beat,
adjusting to yours, so I feel
your every heart beat
pound fast in my chest
when you look at me.

I watch you battle
in your mind between
what you want and need.
I become more powerful
than I have ever been.

But, untethered. Flying
wild and precariously
far out on a strange sea
where there is no safe
place to land.

Intervention in the Mirror

Just walk away.
It ain't happening. Never will.
Just accept it. No matter how pure,
perfect, and passionate.

       No matter how you desire,
       deserve or demand it.

It ain't happening.
Never will. So just shove it down
to the pit of hell, smack it black and blue,
do whatever you must.

       But destroy it. Strangle it.
       Kill it. I don't care.

Because, it ain't happening, never will.
So accept it. Ignore it. Deal with it.
I don't give a shit but, please,
stop thinking about it every goddamn day.

Dear Blue Morpho,

I am done, done with love. It seems a cruel joke. I can't come up with one good reason to keep loving.

Red

Dear Red,

Feel all of it, the passion and the pain. It is our greatest hope, and heaviest burden. Embrace what you are and do what you must. But feel.

Remember, everything you need is already in you.

Blue Morpho

Okay, I am wrecked by love.

Good Question

What would I do
if I trusted
the unknown
parts of me
just as much as I trust
the parts of me
that are known?

Travel
to a distant land
alone,
and allow
myself
to be empty
without burden.

Touching Down in Belize City

I've been waiting
so long to find a place
where I can breathe.

As soon as the wheels
of the plane touched
the Earth in Belize

I felt a fluttering
in my chest,
like a new heartbeat.

With only myself here
I can disappear and heal
my new wound,

my old, jagged scar.

Three Weeks in San Ignacio, Belize

Broken tin fences corral a yard
where mud-colored dogs prowl
among clucking chickens. The smiling
woman clicks her tongue,

calling to the brood to come eat.
She tosses the grains and scraps
and the mutts share the feed bowl
with the fowl. Squawking and growling

to each other in a language
of their making, taking turns,
making time, for each belly to fill.
What kind of love is in this dusty place,

where purpose is more than profit?
Where the smile from a farm
woman earns you the right to call
a strange place home.

There is a peace here that lifts
my soul into view
and fastens my bones
to the Earth.

It is an extraordinary
balance. I never want to leave.

Atop the Pyramid of Cahal Pech

Alabaster skin
against rugged, ancient rock.
I am, in the obvious ways,
misplaced, and yet,

here under the primeval
Mexican sun, I sense
a coming sacrifice of who I am
to the gods of Cahel Pech.

Like a whispering to my soul
from the doorways of the temple
and from the hallways of the sacred
rooms, *"You are remembered."*

It is a comfortable solitude
coaxing me to press my face
against this careful, vetted stone.
It speaks, *"Remember me."*

The touch on my cheek floods
my veins with a euphoria
of reconciliation of my past,
of the choices rendered.

My blood, my bones, my skin relax
as the edge of forgiveness
slices me open, letting loose my demon.
What life was is cast away.

I am left naked, reborn.

A Week in Paradise: Caye Caulker

So many dreams fulfilled, my list grows
by the day including the one that says, "Sit
for hours in the shade of a palm tree doing
nothing, with no intentions, or a single care
to worry the mind, and watch the day
move past you, blissfully slow." Paradise.

The water is so pretty I can't think
when I look into it. I can only submit
to being a part of it. Coming here
was good. Each day brings little to do
and nothing to mind. All that is required
of me is an aimless walk in the wee
morning hours to the East side of the island
to greet the sun. Then in the evening, wander
to the West and watch it go down.

In the middle, is life.

Kathy, a woman I met in San Ignacio, has decided
to stay on here another day. I laughed
when she said she would get on the 10AM boat
back to the mainland today. It is now 3PM.
The last boat of the day has gone
and she is still here. Paradise.

It feels like there is nothing else left in the world,
but this slip of an island and its mangrove beach.

Heaven Happened

In the middle of the sea, on the edge of a beach,
heaven happened to me.

Heaven happened between me and a salty
island breeze snapping my mind free.

Heaven happened by being profoundly filled
with awe while being emptied out.

Heaven happened when I forgot myself, then discovered
my image reflected back to me in a grain of sand.

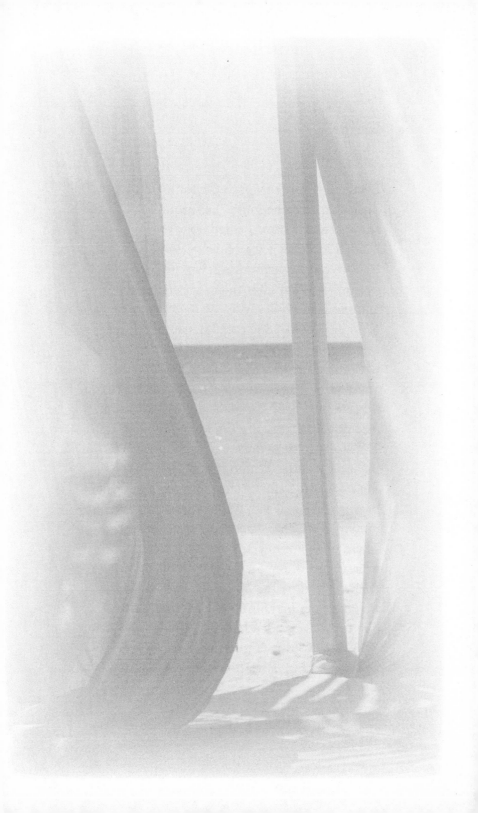

Island Girl

I walked Kathy out onto the long
dock that stretched into the turquoise
sea and to the open bellied boat
headed to Belize City. She was going
back to San Ignacio after trying to leave
five times before. But this is paradise
you see, and no one gets away
from here easily. She eased herself
into the sardine-packed power boat
with the others leaving Caye Caulker
and yelled, "Just think, Kristina. Tomorrow,
this will be you!" I smiled, slightly, knowing
that this was true. My time would come.
Tomorrow, I would have to walk down
the long wooden planks and leave
this enchanted slip of land. But my sarong
blowing in the warm trade winds
reminded me that tomorrow was not today.
There were hours yet to go, and I
was still an island girl, getting a bit more
emancipated by the hour. The sun had streaked
stripes in my hair, and my alabaster glow
had turned a golden hue. I resembled the girl
who came to this land weeks back, but there
was something new about me, resuscitated.

I gave Kathy one more big wave as the boat
moved away. I turned, walked down the dock
to the safety of the mangrove beach,
and to pleasure. Minutes later, I heard a motor
roar. I looked up from collecting seashells,
just in time to watch the boat disappear
into a strange horizon that held another
time, another world.

Last Morning on Caye Caulker

Carlos poured
my last cup
of Belizian coffee
into a mug
with a big smiley
face on it while I sat
on the café porch.

*"So? What did you find during
your adventure to Belize?"* he asked.

I found my peace.

He handed
me the mug
and we watched
the sun break open
on the horizon,
and my heart,
one last time.

*"Is there anything else you need
before you go back home?"*

Yes, a way to stay in peace.

Every chance
you take
unfolds you.
Even though expectation
tries to keep you bound,
remember a seed
must break open
in order to grow.

When you feel
afraid that you
are getting too close
to some edge
of bursting open wide,
it is a good chance
you are right on path.
Keep going.

Back in America

Open, fresh,
and wide-eyed.
Down to the core,
I'm rinsed clean.
I desire again.
I can make fire again.

Dear Blue Morpho,

*Every now and then, I long for a hot Belizean day
and how it felt to slip along the rubble roads, smiling,
my throat parched, sweat catching dust on my skin,
being completely burned out on the afternoon sun.*

*Looking back, I wonder if I knew what was happening
to me while wandering about in plain joyfulness,
contented beyond contentment? Did I realize how easy
it was to release my life and embrace that foreign home?*

*I reminisce often about my time there as I trip along the
path here in America, reworking life. The place still lights
up my face. I am illuminated from the inside out.*

Where are you these days?

Red

Dear Red,

*Beautifully put. It sounds like it was a sweet time.
Traveling to strange lands does soothe the restless soul.*

*Life is humming and bumping along with its usual mixture
of yearning, acceptance, hope, despair, happiness and all
the other human stuff.*

*The muse has been an infrequent visitor to my door these
days. I think it is sort of like love. When you want it so
bad, it never seems to come and even when you have it,
sometimes you long for more. So I await its arrival, the
muse or the more.*

I'm planning a trip to Spain. That is, if they'll have me.

*Have you started that book yet? Or are you living out
more chapters first?*

Still Morphing Blue

A Grand Design

Kissing under a big moon sky and eating
delicious Italian pie bedside, we lay
feeding each other right where we fell

feeling as if, not for one night, but forever,
we had made each other sigh.
Years later, I am still beguiled

by any man's russet eyes. By men
who remind me how to live on the edge,
men who can make me laugh,

and at the same time, cry.
I slip and slide back in my mind
to the moment we found that first kiss

at the seaside. Wishing I knew how to roll
back time, for one more chance, to feel
what I felt that night. I was never the same.

We were never meant to be the same
after sacrificing ourselves to a love
we could never claim, and yet by knowing you

I've found my ability to love has grown.
I would never trade you or the pain
of never knowing you, beyond that night.

Chapter Three

Walking in the Forest

My eyes lift to leaf lines
and glistening spider webs,
the crystallized dew
on a fresh, pine cone edge.
My fingers push deep
into moist muddy roots,
digging through old leaf beds
to find something new.
I hear a woodpecker's knock
and skittering feet,
the scent of the drenched earth
intoxicates me.
Each tiny brilliance
wears a sweet mask
seducing all my senses,
dismantling me,
pulling to pieces and bits
the shackles that bind,
holding me prisoner
to metal, money and time.
Here, I am free,
arms stretched wide,
standing, brave and alone.
Receive me, dear Lord,
I offer my body, my soul.
See me, plant me, feed me,
like I were a seed breaking
open to the sun.

First Meeting

How you'll leave me wondering.
Like a child, I'll feel free,

curious about what new adventure
you'll bring me.

When I'm with you I will know
by reaching out to touch you,

with just the tips of my fingers,
to feel the landscape of your skin.

To kiss? Lips meeting and parting,
exploring each other. In the heat

of that moment I'll be sent reeling.
But, in a touch, one brush

across your cheek, I will discover
a whole, new world.

Dear Blue Morpho,

Love keeps coming and going without me, so I rumble on,
trying to hold my place in this world while I am feeling
it all, every single last drop of it; even when it stings,
especially when it soothes.

I remind myself to feel everything, just feel, and keep
feeling and being OK with the feeling of it all. And when
I think I can't feel any more, I cut myself open a bit further.

I think I am ready for anything, these days.

Still becoming Red

Dear Red,

Love comes and goes and we rumble on. To fall in love again, or to have another fall in love with you, if only for 3 minutes. Ahhh, yes.

Sometimes that is all we need to have our tanks filled and keep us rolling. Life always seems to be about love, and everything else is just, everything else — politics, jobs, writing, watching the grandchildren play.

Yes, talking wise is easy when we disarm ourselves of our own experiences, but really — why do people hide from the reality that what they all want, me included, is to feel love?

I should think a full glass of red wine would be good company to this dribbling. And I think I will go get that good company.

Keep loving, and writing about it. All else is not worth the living.

> *Enjoy,*
> *Blue Morpho*

The natural world
touches my heart
faster than a prayer.

It blows gently
across my skin
and through my hair
like a new lover's fingers.

It sends up tangled in air
the musky scent
of new roots and old growth,
filling my body with reverence.

I am remembered
in the wild like a lost love
come home.

Savoring Desire

Your hand lingers
on my leg.

In this crowded room,
all can see our desire.

Your eyes dance on me,
wondering if I might know

how your heart will feel
beating through your chest

into mine. I lean in for more
and you meet me

with a kiss. Then, you whisper
to me about the rain

coming down, how warm
the night is, that we will

walk home slow,
taking the long way.

I am ready, once more,
to risk everything for love,

and being a woman.

When I'm with him, it is like
a warm wind on my skin.
My soul relaxes, breathes with ease.

He is a home, to me.

Falling Asleep

Our feet tangle, the curve
of my calves against his shins, knees

hitched leading to thighs, mine soft
and supple against his strength.

The perfect joining of his pelvis
against my round flesh slips

elegantly into the length of my back
curling into his lean torso and chest.

One arm beneath and the other slung
over my waist, hand holding

my hand. Our necks parallel, his head
resting along the side of my face, nestled.

I feel his breath easing in and out, washing
over my cheek, as if I were a shore

and he were a gentle sea.

Encounter at the Melon Stand

I reached for a melon.
Your fingers long,
full and capable
ran along its surface
one thumb pressing
lightly to feel
how giving it was.

You took the melon.
I thought you
would crush it,
but your hold was gentle
as you raised it to your face
to breathe in its scent.

I smiled, my hair falling
across my face.
You put the melon
into the cart.
Later that evening,
we ate the melon.
It was fresh, sweet, delicious.

My love, so were you.

I feel like I could stay in the middle
of loving him for the rest of my life.

Is this what lasting love feels like?

Or, must I steady myself
for what will come?

This one may break me open wide, forever.

I Want More

Late afternoon sun
pours through the open
window covering us
with a butter cream hue,
like a summer's blanket.

I watch the tiny hairs
on your arm vibrate
in the wind that blows
into the room, then billows
out the bedroom door,

into the kitchen, where the cats
sleep. A pillow falls
to the floor when we melt
our bodies into one,
and you whisper in my ear.

Great Falls National Park

11:00 AM
I long to be naked here, stripped
down to pale skin and settled
on this hard, hot rock. Baking
in the sun like some wild, redheaded
iguana, arms and legs stretched
and pressed against solid stone.
Instinctually soaking up heat
to stay alive through another night.

1:45 PM
These sights, these sounds, these scents
of the Great Falls wash away
the taut pressure behind my breasts
from the mangled air of the city.
This hard stone, now sweetened
with my sweat, is worn smooth.
An ageless remnant of lost histories,
left by others who've come before me,
and lay in this crook, this rock bed
to dream, to forget, and to remember.

3:33 PM
The day wanes now and my lips
press light against the cooling rock.
Soaked with heat, my mind fantasizes
about this stone skin opening up
and letting me in to know its life, its history.
My fingers wander over its surface
as if this were his back, defined and strong,
Seems it would be much less of a miracle
if this stone let me in, than if he did.

6:35 PM
The rustling leaves wake me
from my feral sleep. At dusk,
I head back to the city,
to the broken streets and sirens.
To another night with him,
a man who, and I am not sure,
but I think may be delivering
me straight into the crux of one
more love lesson I'm to learn.

Coming to Terms

After we broke up
you brought me wine
and cookies, grapefruit
and sweet butter lettuce.

You split a bouquet
of flowers with me.
You met my sister.
You wrote me notes

while you lay in a tent,
in the rain, in the woods.
You told me it was over,
while you fixed my kitchen sink.

When you climbed into bed
and took me in your arms,
you told me that you had tomatoes
for me from your uncle's garden.

And this is how it went for us
from weeks, to months, to years.
We never have said goodbye,
although we've tried so many times.

Relocation

Uncommon love surfaced.
Rising up

from lovemaking,
the death of his brother,

and his new dream.
I adored him

so much I crossed
all known boundaries

to make his life right again.
But who am I to fix it?

Soon I found myself
standing alone

where I could no longer
see him in a place

he would not try to find.
I'm relocated,

like a blip on a radar screen,
suddenly appearing,

a flicker in the dark.

Lately, I find
myself touching
my belly.

It is flat and taut,
still empty
after all these years.

Perhaps, someday
I will
concede,

and accept
it will never fill
with a new breath.

Dear Blue Morpho,

*Costa Rica sounds beautiful. I hope to go there
someday, too.*

*Yes, I am still writing about love and nature and God.
Since we met at the butterfly farm, it seems they are
all blurring into one.*

*Life is good. But after all these years of loving
I am on my own once more. I fear, when it comes to
love, you should just shoot me, let me loose.*

Your friend,

Red

Dear Red,

Don't we all die a little bit for love? Or anything that looks, tastes, feels, walks and acts like love? Even the head that turns our way in the grocery store, just for a twist of an instant, we wonder if there is a chance we would find love again.

We all undergo the hurt, pain, desire, chase, search, to find in another the validation and enhancement of ourselves. It is so beautifully, and tragically, human.

Thank you for sending your poems. They told the story of your last love well. I know the journey of love you described better than I do the answers; and like someone once said, "If you want answers, study math."

But what you have described, Red, that's life. It is living. It is love. You are love. Shoot you? Now, how could I shoot someone so beautifully human, as you?

Plus, you're just starting to get the rhythm of living this life, now that the three have become one.

> *Be well,*
> *Blue Morpho*

I have come to trust that when life appears to be falling apart, it is actually offering a chance to overflow with all you are capable of being.

Reflections While Flying Home

It's been a long time
since I've been home.
The home made of wood
and stone and brick.
The one that smells of my mother's
perfume and holds my father's chair.

There are many
homes. What of the one
that was made of my last
love's long, strong arms
wrapped around me?
He was a fine home I still miss.

There is an old one
that comes to mind,
now and then. It is a fading
glimmer now. A child
that will never be. The boy
across the aisle is so sweet.

He sort of looks like me.
Am I imagining that?
The boy's life afloat
on this aircraft,
his mother and father, and me,
for now, this is our home.

From up here, at 35,000
feet, inching over the Earth
I can see everything. I am
an omnipresent voyeur
of landscapes
dappled with homes.

A witness
to the intricacy
each life
interlaces with another.
From here, it seems impossible
to have enemies.

Within each home
love plays out
all its many faces
of laughing, crying,
creating, dying,
all going on next door,

sometimes inches
away from neighbors.
In a home like one of those
my family waits to welcome
me, a speck
of life speeding by overhead.

We bear on our backs
nothing
but our coming death
and if we are open,
we believe in a home
beyond this one.

So, I wonder why
I bother to long
for a brick or stone house,
or a phantom child.
Or a man,
who once loved me.

Or that I lack
any person,
place or thing,
like a home.
Because here
above the Earth

there is breathing,
and there is hugging.
There is laughing,
and crying.
There is being between here
and arriving there.

There is a choice
to love or
never love again.
Even the man
who may think on me next,
even if he longs to touch me,

hold me, see my smile,
his choice is temporary,
like this life here.
But this now,
this precious present,
is lovingly infinite.

It is all I will embrace.
Not what has gone before,
or what will be, or what I lack.
We are held, whether we sense
it or not, the boy, his parents,
and me.

Chapter Four

There is always time for a good resurrection.

Manifesto for One

On reflection, here is my
response to all of you:

I will no longer try to figure it out,
or try to get my shit together.

I will not think straight, settle
down, or smile more - or less.

I will not be less emotional,
look perfect, or ever be close to perfect.

I will not be more careful,
less unpredictable,

or stay home and wait for anything.
What I will do is love.

And, love everything
this life brings.

If that is not enough,
I will love myself anyway,

and most of all.

At Pretty Boy Dam

After, long hours of steadfast hiking,
over rock and trail,

I've found this hidden place
tucked in at the edge of gathering waters.

At Pretty Boy's feet
the air sweetens with tannin,

a scent soothing my body,
calming my blood.

Leaving the past dead
at the trailhead,

my wish for oblivion
from what will not be, is complete.

I am free from all that troubled me,
like shedding skin, it falls away.

Now, I dangle my feet in fresh pools
of deep water, feeding on the balm of nature

anointing my skin. I'm becoming
a budding ornament for the Earth to wear.

My heart beats like on the day
I was born, strong and unexpectant.

I revel in deserved bliss; the kind that comes naturally, without effort. It is not such a big secret that force and power are two different natural entities.

Using force to get more of life takes great effort and is draining. Power, however, is a gentle persuasion of pure intention sent into the world.

Be powerful and life will pour bliss all over you.

These Poems

Though always unfinished,
a poem remains whole
even as it is delivered
by her pain or pleasure,

fragments, on an open page.
Where one word appears
followed by another,
creating a line, then two,

and soon a poem forms
to takes its first breath.
She will dote over a word
play with a phrase,

spend sleepless nights
reworking a metaphor.
She will worry
about its readiness.

She will hold it close
where no one can see,
until one day she finds
the poem stands

on its own, able
to carry its meaning
beyond the page, without her.
And she lets it go.

This Tea, the Poet's Words and Me

His eyes steamed
like this tea, enriched

with wisdom won
from years gone by.

I could lie coiled
like a cat at his feet

and listen to the low drumbeat
of his voice tell tales

of learning to live his life
by always stepping to the edge.

I wonder, as age blushes
every edge of my face

if my own eyes
are deepening to a blue-green hue

like a boundless, rolling sea
capable of holding life's mysteries?

I am steeped in possibility
of my half-life turning whole.

Sipping his words between my lips
into my soul.

I'll stumble across him; the one who has lived much like me. The one who shares my truth that love never makes mistakes, but rather provides a life worth living.

Perhaps, I will know him by the natural way he sees more than the pieces and parts of me, but how he takes me in, whole. Enfolding in his arms all I bring to him from my life.

And we will tell each other everything.

Birth, One Hundred Times Over

My womb has never stretched, my body
has never been burdened by labor
or the synapses in my mind snapped
into pathways of protective feral instincts.

But my heart has known the joy
of conceiving a way to live, and the anguish
of realizing I must let that life go
without me into the world.

I have known the burden of incubating
a creative spirit like a caterpillar
blooms a butterfly, and felt its struggle
to release into a strange new phase of life.

After everything I thought my life
would be, never was, I learned how to live
with grace. While being stretched,
burdened, snapped, and crossing boundaries,

even childbirth, to become the woman
I was always meant to be. A woman
who may never be a mother to a child,
but conceives herself one hundred times over.

New Vows

I will take this moment to shine,
to let loose the pent up mystic energy,
and all the mystery infused in my veins
from lifetimes of lineage and ancestry.

I will take this moment to expand, to explode
into the world from the subterranean place
where wisdom resides beholding the absolute,
lovely humor in this human condition.

I will take this moment to love, to be
with you deeply and with more purpose
than a hand on cheek but with open, on fire, desire
flooding us in each second of union.

I will take this moment to laze,
to come to a deliberate and pondering stop
wherever I am and notice all that is asking
nothing of me, but to simply witness it, breathing.

I will take this moment.

Good Life

Let me dive from a cliff
into the deep ocean blue.

Let me cut through the waves
like a blade swift and true.

Let me soar like a bird
through the strong undertow.

Let me sink like a stone
to the sand bottom floor.

Let me sit like a monk
in the silence of the sea.

Let me breathe like a fish
as I pray in the deep.

Let me find a new way
to live on the land.

Let me know how it feels
to hold life in my hands.

Like a child may I live
as these years take their toll.

When I die may I laugh
having lived well with my soul.

The secret love keeps
is that there is no secret at all,
only love.

Homecoming

Let your heart open!
  Let wisdom spring
    up from your heart

out the top
  of your head,
    fall over your shoulders,

down your back,
  spill onto the floor,
    and seep

into every corner
  of your life.
    Feel everything

that is contained
  in your lovely skin,
    not just the collection

of bones and veins
  and muscles,
    but your infinite,

fluid capacity to love.
  Look in the mirror
    and ask, "What is the one

thing left to do
  that will quench
    the rumbling of my heart?"

and do it.
  Be your own quest
    to come alive.

Set out with nothing
  but the bravery
    to seek yourself,

invite the world to know you,
  and live without fear.
    Then, you will be home.

Everywhere.

Dear Blue Morpho,

I am in a holding pattern above a life I am ready to let go of. Waiting to know which direction to go . . .

I've started to compile my book of life, of love. It is difficult to relive so many memories and to finish it seems an endless journey, but I'm in the middle of it now and there is no turning back. It is what I must do.

Seems something larger than my one life has finally taken hold.

Always Becoming Red

Dear Red,

I love the honesty, "I am in a holding pattern, ready to let go."

Sometimes directions are crosses we've picked up to bear for someone else and we don't know how to put them down, anymore. I know all too well about this. Maybe you are better off drifting, living lightly. Find out what is really important to you, even if only for a moment. What is important to you now is not going to be important later, so enjoy the things that make you happy, at whatever stage of life.

I feel like I'm writing a note to myself, which I guess, I always am. I have an urge to hit the road again. Find new eyes. Pack up whatever seems essential, and go.

Directions can sometimes be over-rated. May be best just to strike out in any direction with your new way of living. I think you are ready for life to find you.

Forever Morphing Blue

*Life is falling into place, the top layers cleanly
peeled away to reveal yet an ever deeper core,
with its own evolution I've yet to flow through.*

*I've arrived in a place where breathing
is easier, and what comes and goes does just that.
I await the next wave of life, in peace.*

The Tapestry

Silken strands,
one over another,
then merged with a third,
who takes the threads
now and spins them
into a design
of my life?

Born from love
I have lived
leaving some distant master
at the loom.
The maker of me,
a work of art
in progress.

But, as the years
spin by
more and more
the loom's chair
sits
empty,
becoming mine.

How my heart
soars as I add
a new weave
of violet

or indigo
or swirling
scalloping arcs.

Or seam
curling ribbons
of viridian
and sienna,
falling
into elegant pools
of burnished gold.

Some where
some place,
some god
watches
and smiles
as I choose
a new thread,

mesh it
into another,
giving myself
a new twirl, color,
or shade of light,
learning, at last, to live
the life dreamed for me.

Lessons Learned, so far

Free yourself every day.
Check out, often. It's OK.

Feast on you.
Your beauty,
your wounds,
your willingness.

Discover silence.
Fear no one.
Calm down. Rest. Then play.
Feel everything.

Pay attention.
Be in love with your life, first.

The number of years a woman has, what we call age,
bears no regard to her being in the "prime" of life.

When in her prime, a woman experiences calm
confidence in mind, she enjoys purposeful action
in body and she respects her capacity to express
the whole spectrum of emotions with grace.

She flows.

This sensibility and sensuality comes and goes
throughout her life if she finds her rhythm.
Many women never realize this and they end up
growing old and thinking their prime is over,
when it is only waiting to be born again.

On Fire

When you bear
first witness
to your own
vulnerability
and accept love,
in all its forms,
without judgment.

When you confess
to yourself first,
all your transgressions,
before you ask forgiveness
from another.
When you dig,
plummet

to the origin
of the first time
you lived your truth,
before the world
stepped in
and chose truth
for you.

When you sacrifice
your life to a belief
in something larger
than life.
When you transcend
beyond adversity
rising up

from a buried past
then, you receive
the gift
of being belly
soft, and welcoming.
Then, you can invite
into your heart

the ecstasy of love
along with the sharp
edges of this world
to know you.
You will be led
to what you must do,
and you will do it.

Even in the face
of destruction,
by those who would choose
to diminish you,
you go the distance
to build a life
of your own.

Releasing
all that was once
your silence
walking naked
in the world,
for the first time
on fire with your truth.

Whole Woman I Am

These tiny lines blessing
the edges of my face
prove my time spent
in the world, where mistakes
brought forth more mistakes,
or grew wisdom.
My presence stirs, flowing
into a harmonious rhythm
with all that comes, goes,
and may or may never be.

One day, I will look
into deeper lines
that have come to decorate
me and know each was well
earned by summoning
that presence born in deep
waters, smoldering
with passionate grace
offering the constant
comfort to share
with the world
the whole woman I am.

*One day you may wake up and know your life
is only a small part of an existence far beyond
the scope of your understanding.*

*It is then you may begin to appreciate breathing
for the first time, and you may even discover
the courage to live the life you were meant for.*

Live.

Dear Red,

I see you've surfaced once more to let the world know you are alive and well. It was good to get the news of your book. Ahh, what an honorable journey you've made.

It is never about the way, or the style or the tempo with which a person lives, it is about the fact that she does; that she feels, she feels all of it, every single last drop.

The greatest gift we can give ourselves is a life we can die away from, with ease.

I am off to Nepal in the morning. I must go.

Always Blue Morpho

P.S. Have you ever wondered what a butterfly morphs into next when it's done being a butterfly?

Do me a favor and let me know . . .

Red Butterfly

I am to be left wild in the world,
            childless,
            childlike,
            passionate,
            determined,
            and free.
Emboldened by the new
and courageous to strike out
even where the road ends.

Fearless in confession,
and comforted, despite
how vast and alone the world
can feel. Able to hold pleasure
and pain as the same gift.

Ready to turn a corner
and greet the new adventure
that will further reveal
my soul's work. Loving
beyond measure, laughing

beyond breath, feeling
all highs and depths, and dying
only when completely used up.
My spirit returning once more,
to swirl into the dancing whirl
            of God's
            grand
            underflow.

The real adventure
is living each day knowing
you will step out
on the edge, peer over,
and leap into the unknown
of love,
of being
able to feel
everything.

Open, open to the flow . . .

Acknowledgments

*"It takes a village of fabulous people
to bring a first book into the world."*
—Kristina Mercier

First and foremost I want to thank my parents, 3 sisters and brother, their spouses, and their 11 beautiful children. You are the foundation of my life.

I would like to thank all the men and women, too many to list, with whom I've shared loving and lasting friendships.

To the men I've loved, love is always beautiful.

I would like to thank my grandparents, now passed, who remind me daily to live to a life I can die away from with ease.

Special thanks goes out to all the people who held the manuscript of this book in their hands along the way:

Todd Feldman, your words inspired me to compile my writing into book form. First readers: Heidi Craun and Pamela Pfeiffer. You were my original readers who encouraged me to press on in the creation of this book. Vicki Macchione, you gave it structure and strength. Christine Stewart, you always urge me to dig deeper as a writer. Linda Strommer for helping me to understand the publishing world.

My Superstar Team of Experts:
Dorie McClelland – Interior Designer
Peri Poloni-Gabriel – Cover/Interior Designer
Kate McMillan – Website Designer
Gail Kearns – Book Shepherd

Thank you for your unshakable support, the women of CIRA: Sue Nodine, Deborah Van DeGrift, Janet O'Neil and Pamela Pfeiffer.

Loving Gratitude goes to Tricia Defibaugh and Jeni Biehn
Thank you for believing in *An Agreement with Love* with an amazing energy that can make dreams come true.

About the Author

KRISTINA MERCIER
was born and raised in the small town of Flushing,
Michigan. At the age of ten, she began writing daily.
It has been her great passion to write powerfully, but
simply, about life, love and Nature. Currently, she
makes her home in Baltimore, Maryland where she
shares living space with two mercurial felines.

Follow her at:
www.kristinamercier.com or
www.anagreementwithlove.com